MW01013333

This journal belongs to

DRAW
near to
GOD

COLORING
JOURNAL

ILLUSTRATED BY
NATASHA BHAGWANANI

The Lord Bless You & Keep You.

NUMBERS 6:24 NKJV

YOUR PROMISES HAVE BEEN THOROUGHLY TESTED; THAT IS WHY I LOVE THEM SO MUCH.

PSALM 119:140 NLT

If I rise on the wings of dawn,
If I settle on the far side of the sea,
Even there your hand will guide me,
Your right hand will hold me fast.

Psalm 139:9-10 NIV

MAY the GOD of HOPE FILL YOU WITH ALL Joy & Peace AS YOU TRUST IN HIM, SO THAT YOU MAY Overflow with Hope.

ROMANS 15:13 NIV

It is good for ME to draw near to GOD.

PSALM 73:28 NKJV

SHOW ME YOUR WAYS
O LORD;
TEACH ME YOUR PATHS.
PSALM 25:4 NKJV

TRUST IN THE
LORD
WITH ALL YOUR
HEART...
AND HE SHALL
DIRECT YOUR
PATHS.

PROVERBS 3:5-6 NKJV

YOU, O LORD, ARE GOOD & FORGIVING.

PSALM 86:5 ESV

This only do I seek: that I may DWELL in the house of the LORD all the days of my LIFE.

PSALM 27:4 NIV

If God cares so wonderfully for wildflowers... he will certainly care for you.

MATTHEW 6:30 NLT

I am always with you.

PSALM 73:23 NIV

Draw near to GOD and He will draw near to YOU.

JAMES 4:8 NKJV

Satisfy us in the MORNING with your unfailing LOVE.

PSALM 90:14 NIV

I will bless you... and you shall be a blessing.

GENESIS 12:2 NKJV

If you abide in ME, and my words abide in YOU, ASK WHATEVER YOU WISH, AND IT WILL BE DONE FOR YOU.
JOHN 15:7 ESV

The Lord is
gracious & compassionate,
slow to anger & rich in love.

PSALM 145:8 NIV

Delight Yourself in the Lord; and He will give you the desires of your heart. PSALM 37:4 NASB

The LORD himself will fight for you.

EXODUS 14:14 NLT

Every good and perfect gift is from above, coming down from the FATHER of the heavenly LIGHTS, who does not change like shifting shadows.

JAMES 1:17 NIV

God is Our REFUGE & STRENGTH, an ever-present help in trouble.

PSALM 46:1 NIV

GIVE,
and it will be
given to you.

LUKE 6:38 NIV

"For I know the plans I have for you,"
declares the Lord,
"plans to prosper you and
not to harm you, plans to give
you hope and
a future."

JEREMIAH
29:11 NIV

The fruit OF the SPIRIT is Love, Joy, Peace, PATIENCE, KINDNESS, goodness, FAITHFULNESS, gentleness, Self-Control.

GALATIANS 5:22-23 ESV

YOUR FATHER Knows Exactly WHAT YOU NEED EVEN BEFORE YOU ASK HIM!

MATTHEW 6:8 NLT

THE LORD IS MY Strength & MY Shield;

MY Heart TRUSTED IN Him, AND I AM HELPED.

PSALM 28:7 NKJV

The Lord is my Shepherd;
I shall not want.
He makes me to lie down in green pastures;
He leads me beside the still waters.
He restores my soul.

PSALM 23:1-3 NKJV

Don't worry about anything; instead, pray about everything.

PHILIPPIANS 4:6 NLT

I am convinced that nothing can ever separate us from God's love.

ROMANS 8:38 NLT

God can do ANYTHING YOU KNOW— far more than you COULD EVER IMAGINE OR GUESS OR REQUEST IN YOUR WILDEST DREAMS! EPHESIANS 3:20 MSG

The steadfast LOVE of the LORD never ceases, his mercies never come to an end; they are new every morning; great is your faithfulness.

LAMENTATIONS 3:22-23 ESV

WHERE YOUR TREASURE is, there your HEART will be also.

MATTHEW 6:21 NKJV

May you be BLESSED by the LORD, THE MAKER OF HEAVEN & EARTH.

PSALM 115:15 NIV

BE
Strong
&
Courageous!
DO NOT TREMBLE
OR BE DISMAYED,
for the Lord your God
IS WITH YOU
WHEREVER
YOU GO.

JOSHUA 1:9 NASB

LET ALL THAT I AM PRAISE THE LORD; MAY I NEVER FORGET the good things he does for me.

PSALM 103:2 NLT

They who wait for the Lord
shall renew their
Strength;
they shall mount up
with wings like eagles;
they shall run and not be weary;
they shall walk and not faint.

ISAIAH 40:31 ESV

Ellie Claire® Gift & Paper Expressions
Franklin TN, 37067
Ellie Claire is registered trademark of Worthy Media, Inc.

Draw Near to God Coloring Journal
© 2016 by Ellie Claire

Art © 2016 by Natasha Bhagwanani
Designed by Bart Dawson
Published by Ellie Claire, an imprint of Worthy Publishing Group, a division of Worthy Media, Inc.

ISBN 978-1-63326-138-9

Scripture quotations taken from: The Holy Bible, New International Version®, NIV® Copyright © 1973, 1978, 1984, 2011 by Biblica, Inc.® All rights reserved worldwide. The Holy Bible, English Standard Version® (ESV®), copyright © 2001 by Crossway Bibles, a publishing ministry of Good News Publishers. THE MESSAGE (MSG). Copyright © 1993, 1994, 1995, 1996, 2000, 2001, 2002. Used by permission of NavPress Publishing Group. All rights reserved. The New King James Version® (NKJV). Copyright © 1982 by Thomas Nelson. Used by permission. Holman Christian Standard Bible® (HCSB) Copyright © 1999, 2000, 2002, 2003, 2009 by Holman Bible Publishers. Used with permission by Holman Bible Publishers, Nashville, Tennessee. All rights reserved. Scripture taken from the NEW AMERICAN STANDARD BIBLE® (NASB), Copyright © 1960, 1962, 1963, 1968, 1971, 1972, 1973, 1975, 1977, 1995 by The Lockman Foundation. Used by permission. *Holy Bible*, New Living Translation (NLT), copyright © 1996, 2004, 2015 by Tyndale House Foundation. Used by permission of Tyndale House Publishers Inc., Carol Stream, Illinois 60188. All rights reserved.

Excluding Scripture verses and deity pronouns, in some quotations references to men and masculine pronouns have been replaced with gender-neutral or feminine references. Additionally, in some quotations we have carefully updated verb forms and wording that may distract modern readers.

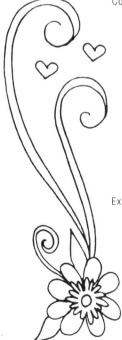

Printed in the United States
2 3 4 5 6 7 8 9 – 21 20 19 18 17 16